Rooms for Rent in the Burning City

Cover design by Jen Lambert
Cover Art courtesy of Brandon Colaprete

Book design by Jen Lambert

ISBN 978-0-9897837-2-9

Published by Spark Wheel Press

Rooms for Rent in the Burning City

Brandon Courtney

Spark Wheel Press, Omaha, NE

For Benjamin Johnson and Vincent Parker

Antechamber

The Roman Room

The Crying Room

Acknowledgements

The Author

Antechamber

Controlled Burn

How little I know of fire
watching flames
raze the neighboring farmhouse
to cinders.

Deserted for decades,
flames shivered from blue
sparks into black ringlets of soot,
severed the roof in two—
like the high school girl,
muscled inside the house's
humid storm cellar.

Knifeless, liquored boys
pinned her wrists,
took turns,
one after another,
until her pain was no longer pain,
until her body
was a kind of fluency
in their native hands,
until the sky
inside her lungs was starless.

Then they disappeared
into illegible darkness.
& because there is nothing
in this world
cleaner than ash, the fire

department lit a retributive blaze,
watched fire walk
its slow course
through the kitchen, hallways.

Those who were there
& saw it burn
will one day see it again: a month
from now, a year—
embers having grown cold
as wet stones—
each time they drive the gravel
past the empty acre.

Which means the flames,
somehow, go on living
in memory, mending the world
with some bright nothing.
which could have been her name,
if they'd thought, at all,
to gift her one.

& now, if you listen for her voice,
it will sound like fruit
bats flowering from abandoned silos,
which is the sound
revenge makes as it drills
into nothing.

There are gods & there are boys:
I knew one, once, whose father,
bored with ordinary bodies,
took him to the only porno theater
left in town & how years later,
still believing love
was something urgent & brutal,
held a drill-bit to a teenaged girl's throat,
unblessing her body with his.

He must have thought he could get away
with it. Or get away, at least,
from the name, light as the bandage
his father wrapped around his life,
away from the theaters—
where for five bucks
teenaged boys could finally see
full frontal: women tall as dark trees,
bearing a simpler fruit.

He told me once—
moments before the projectionist
loaded the black spools—that he felt his soul
leave his body. He didn't mean soul,
exactly, but whatever it is that departs us
& enters lifeless things, which means
a part of him is still there
in the plush seat, red as a newborn's lungs,
mistaking the smell of popcorn
for burnt hair.

MEMORANDUM FOR THE RECORD: EVIDENCE/PROPERTY CUSTODY RECEIPT

End:

1) Chronological Record of Medical Care (SF600) ICO The Human Remains that are believed to be Petty Officer Third Class Benjamin A. Johnson, USN, 090-64-2820 of 23 Nov 01

2) The purpose of this memorandum for the record is to document the following facts regarding the subject's human remains:

   a) Received custody from LT Mat Kerver, HC Detachment on or about 1630 on this date.

   b) The only personal effects received were:

      i) Wallet containing
1. Geneva Conventions Identification Card (DD Form 2)
2. Department of the Navy Gemplus Identification Card
3. Blockbuster Rewards Card
4. AT&T Phone Card
5. Cyber Zone Card
6. AAA Card Plus RV in name of Stacie Haas
7. Value+ Phone Card; $20.00
8. Verizon Calling Card
9. A believed to be foreign note for 1000 Dinar
10. HSBC Card
11. Barnes & Noble Reader's Advantage Card
12. New York Driver's License

      ii) Contents of Miscellaneous Written Notes: All notes are transcribed in original form
1. Note 1: Dreamt that a girl followed me from the subway on 169th to Briarwood until she realized I wasn't her brother. She had broken glass in her hair & started crying because she was lost.
2. Note 2: Dreamt last night that there was a lobby of young girls dressed in yellow at the Hotel Giraffe, resplendent light coming off the East River. I stood at the bar reading the Sunday paper.

3. Note 3: Dreamt of white dwarfs falling in Brooklyn Heights, of fireflies in mason jars, rusted silverware, warm milk, transistor radios, women's breath & kookaburras in Queens.
4. Note 4: Dreamt of the recent snow in Columbus Park where I went from antique shop to antique shop looking for my father's 1967 Underwood typewriter.
5. Note 5: Dreamt early this morning that traffic was stopped along the Williamsburg Bridge; I watched the pedestrian traffic throw dead sparrows into the East River.
6. Note 6: Best dream of New York since the deployment. I dreamt that I stopped & watched Oscar Peterson play in a bar between West 10th and Fifth, by NYU. After the performance, Oscar & I went to a delicatessen on 12th & drank coffee where I burned the roof of my mouth.
7. Note 7: Dreamt of riding the Thunderbolt rollercoaster on Coney Island. Although I was young when they tore it down, there were small fires in the wood framing, but the structure never fell. A man walking the beach offered to sell me a portrait of Stacie & me together,   even though she wasn't there.
8. Note 8: Dreamt of a black chalkboard in the basement of a church, a Sunday school room in Brooklyn, with the word "Jesus" written in cursive.

iii) The personal effects listed on enclosure were not received.
   1. 9 Millimeter Handgun
   2. Two Ammo Clips
iv) All miscellaneous notes have been hermetically sealed & shipped with remains.

Shamal

—after Marvin Bell

"A shamal had been developing throughout the night. The winds had increased 3o to 4o knots & the seas were 8 to 1o feet. [...] We received a call from the USS Peterson that MV Samra was capsizing in the heavy seas. The crew & security team were preparing to abandon ship. [...] We were told a few minutes later the ship had gone down, & all 22 people were in the water." *—Dave Bouve*

Of the captain, Nakhoda Yekom, I remember his teeth,
Van Gogh-yellow like orchids
blown between rows of cotton stocks, & his uniform,
his arrow point collar, the fabric's Venetian blonde weave:
the color & texture of boxwood grain.

Of the Nasarvan's forearms, I remember the sallow
shapes of his brother's name—the Farsi method
of tattooing: patterns razored into skin, incisions kneaded
with black ash from the funeral pyre.

Of the Navban Dovom's Kalashnikov, I remember
the slight bank of the banana clip, the polished
butt of the weapon pressed hard against his clavicle, & the scar
he showed me, pulling the collar off his shoulder: a pink
night crawler stretched across travertine.

Of the Navi Yekom, even less—only the slow pull on
a smuggled Cuban bent between his lips, ash as long
& true as his index finger.
Of the Navi Dovom—my same age & equivalent rank—
I remember the sewing needle he used to drain the blisters

on both heels, & his parade boots, how he practiced
tying deck-knots with the laces: bowline, reef, & timber-
hitch before a full-length mirror.

Of the shamal, I remember the sudden swell of waves,
the yarn of sea kraits washed aboard the weather decks
before capsizing, a hundred snakes, motionless, unable
to move on land or this steel island.

For provisional lifeboats, some men folded their bodies
over the curve of crude-oil canisters. I used the buoyancy
of the Nakhoda Yekom's bloated body.

[Misreading] The Odyssey in Iraq

Years spent in weariness, shipwrecked on the Isle of Iraq.

> [I misread Nausikaa's unholy movements—
> she of white arms—as drowning swanlings
> in glassine water, wave-wracked, spreading
> their blemish-rinsed feathers wing-tip-to-wing-tip
> on sandbanks.]

She sinks, instead, pale sails of linen; her strange body
is havocked as flight, anointed with golden oil for softening
girls, into the shattering river.

> [I mistake it for the lordly Tigris, undrinkable Euphrates.]

She is content, now, to gaze into its ambulate mirror,
to white, like capsized ships, the water
with sheeting.

Artemis gathers her arrows, thunderstroked
into the curving earth, ghosting
deer.

> [I misread their skin as immaculate,
> albinal, & not as bone-wreathed bucks, haunting
> the underwood.]

Odysseus rises—a reed from silt—to kneel at Nausikaa's
knees as if they were fire, altar.
Ramadi greens through night vision goggles.

[I mistake a soldier for the mountain
lion, Odysseus — brine-armored, wind-crippled,
prowling door-to-door, M-116 laser-scoped
on hijabed women suspected of veiling men
& their suicide belts in spider holes.]

Baghdad has burned a year longer than Troy.

[I mistake its ash, wide as a grown man's palm, elephant's
ear, for Icarus, falling a thousand times back to earth.]

Achilles, Veterans' Hospital

—Philadelphia, Pennsylvania

Because his pain's no longer phantom,
he traces two fingers along the scar
where surgeons went looking for a lion,
opened the bone cage of his chest.

He waits in the emergency room's
borrowed light for orderlies to drag
his corpse behind the wheelchair's shadow,
knowing doctors will make peace

with his parts. His greaves have been
replaced with gauze, cuirass for paper
gown, mitra for colostomy bag.
He knows how an august father could perch

on a son's shoulders, grip the wick
of his neck, as they both flee the burning city.

After War, I Park Outside a Local Bar & Do Not Go Inside

           The heart suffers
its hundred eruptions;
the world is not so different.

I think tonight I'll go back
to my old ways: hatred
         of an hour, inebriety,

back to the dark parts
of some midwestern city,
         to the whiskey bars

that blast 80's ballads
from two blown speakers,
         where blood rises

to meet the tongues of women,
willing, singing, who need
no invitation to stain

a stranger's sheets. It's all lost
on me now, this give & take
         of another's touch.

My hands are decades removed
from anything so beautiful.
I think tonight I'll go back
         to those old memories.
I need only to close my eyes
to remember her
         in another's bed,

in a strange city made of cold
glass, to remember horses
by the highways
            huddled against snow.

I know, now, that lust requires
an understanding of distance:
desire carries a body out of itself,

farther. & she was right
to seduce a softer lover. I have
not used this anger well.

Like a Thousand Things Still in Flight

      Because it still amazes me
to think that I can see

      no further than the high-rise
behind you, the forgery

      of sky lifted from gallery
walls, the autumn leaves

      like traffic lights oscillating
green, then yellow, then red,

      in the updraft of alleyways,
in the parking lot's dark

      anatomy. Consider the house
key you broke in the lock

      of your body a blessing. No
more will boys vanish

      from your field, than call it
standing alone in a landscape.

      No more will boys write your
name in chalk, erase it

      with their hands, & clap you
into dust.

Invasion

This grief isn't mine
alone: the fall
        after returning

from war,
asleep beside my wife,
        a bat—

appeared suddenly
in our room, stalked

mosquitoes,
while sulpher moths
        knocked

against the bulb's
remaining flicker—
        it circled

& circled & fed
until landing
on our north wall,
        trembling.

All the soldier does
after war is done
        with violence:

I crushed
the black bruise

of its body
      with my hands

before my wife could
open the window
      or find a broom.

After, I washed
my nails
      then fed

on my wife's fingers
& breasts,
      swallowing

her breath
until she, too, fell,
      saying to me:

with you
I have never felt
      so safe,

saying to herself:
I no longer know you;
I've never been
      so afraid.

After War, I Imagine Killing the Marine Who Slept With My Wife

It's with the claw-end
of a carpenter's hammer.
                  I imagine a lake

where the moon's reflection
splinters, its light pounded
                  straight as a nail

through black water,
which makes it more real.
So, too, the smell of beer

& bourbon still whispering
its small breath
                through his pores

like an apology,
a plea, as I drag his body
through loam

           & underbrush
by the ankles.
We're almost to the site

where river meets shore,
almost to the shallows
where I imagine

           a fisherman,
months from now, casting
a fly rod into the lake.

He'll mistake the man's mandible
for that of an animal's,
      mistake his pose

for a dosing sleeper.
Open up & show me
      your bones;

there's no escaping
the hammer's dumb weight
in this otherwise

soundless landscape,
the faraway birds
      flying in the wakes

of their own ugly songs.
I'll know my muscles
      not by their names,

but how they burn
      with the labor of digging
his insignificant grave.

On Seeing My Ex-Wife at the Farmers' Market

Bent over wooden crates,
your hands dipped
                        into a season

of Arkansas Blacks,
Autumn Golds, you finger
            the bruises

where the pulp has gone
mealy, press
            where its flesh

hurts the most.
You've never touched me
            like the apples

you're holding now,
never lifted any part of me
to your nose, your lips,

& inhaled as wholly,
deeply, as you do
            with the Asian pears;
the white onions'

tunics look like your wedding
gown's tattered neckline.
            Darling, the red bell
pepper you're palming
            looks like the ghost

of a heart. I made a room,
once, in those very hands.
        In the end,
don't we learn by touching

the skin, don't most things
        breathe

through the smallest
             of openings?
Everything you taught
me about leaving
        tells me to distrust
the sudden stillness

of the soft-edged
pomegranate
& its hundred hearts within.

Petrified Lightning

        Last night, a combat
veteran—dishonorably
discharged

for gracefully breaking
a Budweiser bottle
across another's face—

    called to tell me his wife
had filed for divorce
       & driven

their newborn daughter
across state lines.
He, drunk and naked,
                crying,

had blacked out
in the nursery's rocker,
           lullabying

their child to sleep.
He called to tell me
that after years
       on solid ground

he could still feel
the movement of water
beneath his feet.
Mother to nothing,
       we exhausted

years ago the idea
of conceiving,
                    bent as we were

on hollowing each other.
Now, late snow
whitens the spare room,
the books I've neglected
            to read, shelved,
against the unfinished wall:
ocean blue. Baby blue.

When I open the book
            of weather, I learn
that sand becomes glass,

a river cut by light,
                    rare as gold,
as heat spirals sand
                    around sand.

Meiosis

Back, once again, to those silent hours,
our only daughter having since fallen

asleep, exhausting her cry in another
room. The needle lifts from a 45, slow

guitar, slow guitar, last rattle and hum
of hi-hat, kettledrum. The patron

saint of music ghosts the room, lowing
her harpsichord afterworld. The house

is still with sleep's litany; two dark syllables
sit like horse pills on our tongues, whisper

divorce, divorce. How human, division—
this room-to-room meiosis: mine, yours,

this bed, gold ring, this hour. There's never
time for another song, never time enough.

Dodge & Burn

October, familiar wounds surface
on the cover of the *Post*—
a soldier's hands lifted
                        towards a hive

of gauze. His fingers are ten
stingless bees. Say *bomb*,
                        & we'll both see

different explosions; I see a man
blown into the landscape
                        of his own shadow.

Nightly, I paint
the ceiling of my skull
                        with his image.

A Blind Date Asks About the War

How should I answer her
question, *did you kill*
            anyone overseas?

I tell her this: a man aimed
more than his rifle
            at my chest;

he aimed
the possibility
            of nothingness
& death.

His hands
were the most familiar
            weapons he carried;

            he made them
into a hundred things
            more: shovels, cradle,

& blindfolds.
            These were his alone.
I tell her this:

If you walk a mile
in any direction
            you're bound
to meet the dead,
buried in soft
            mattresses of soil.

36

Wind will move
the graveside grass like hair

underwater. I tell her
this: how the green blades
stir is only half
            of my answer.

Bow & Cello

I.

Once, lost in the Museum of London,
I sat in the war, plague, & fire
gallery, watching a woman

step slowly back from an oil painting.
The city's great fire —
Saint Paul's Cathedral biblical
in its destruction — as if the flames

were real &, in their certainty,
threatened to raze
the grand hall to ash.

A child clung to the hem of her dress.
As if warming them,
he held both palms to the painting, surprised

to find only the room's coolness.
Perspective doesn't give perspective.
We deserve the knowledge

that, separately, horses asleep
beneath spruce in the rain do little
more than pepper the fields
with their darkness, but together make
bow & cello. & the child
who thought to warm his fingers
against a depiction of fire
—we deserve him, too.

II.

Just a month underway,
the sailors had searched
      out shadowed vestibules,

isolated engine rooms
where the whine of turbines
      drowned the moans a throat
      invents for orgasm.

In a boiler room
humid with steam
I watched, unnoticed,
a man make love to a woman,
      young, boyish

I thought, by her hair combed
      into a bun.

She suffered him:
Sweat stinking like old coins,
the pressure,
      the pain of it all.

She mouthed
the word motherfucker
to herself, or to him,
      or some idea of him
outside of history.
Or maybe she meant
to curse airplanes, the towers
      that collapsed

with a believer's flare
for kneeling & brought her
      here, brought me here.
At nineteen,
      what did they know
of the body?

At nineteen, they knew
everything the living
      know.

Memento Mori

There are some things too sacred to teach
but, tonight, I'm home from war & the butcher

demonstrates the perfect cut: medallions
of Iberico so thin I can see the silvered blade

through each sliver. He buries bone spike in hock,
lifts calla to his nose, claims to smell the acorns

on which it feasted, the trees' roots, the black lake
from which the hog drank. I'll believe anything.

In a country I'll never see, tribesman turn corpses
into wine: particles of bone picked from the ashes

of cremation fires, ground with corn; the body
rests in the simple box of another's body.

Once, I watched a coroner prep an open casket
for a soldier. He trimmed the hair, cut short

the fingernails, washed the skin. Because war breaks
the hearts of men, I no longer believe

dirt deserves our dead. When only bone remains,
the butcher says, find the bluest vein & drink.

Jesus Dreamt Only Once

He stepped into the sea,
smelled the crushed odor
of weeds, knew thirst

for the first time,
the compulsion to drink,
& drink of it his fill.

He prayed for mercy
& mercy came
in the shape of waves, crushing

Capernaum to sand, floating
the sternum of his body
like an empty boat.

He dreamt the sea kneeling
at the entrance of his mouth,
swells that unstrung

the necklace of breath
from his throat, beating
their gospels against his ribs.

He dreamt of his Father's coffin.
Just yesterday, men were bathing
in it, spitting, moving
through it, swimming,
pressed as close as the bones
of a wrist.

& for the first time,
He heard his Father's voice,
            swallowed like the blade

of an oar, tongue swollen,
            black, filling his mouth,
the dark hymns cast like nets.

He dreamt of salt burning
in the beaks of birds,
                their jaws atrophied

in an arch of praise, the sea
giving up her dead, the corruptible
bodies swaddled in sailcloth,

white flotilla—
there & there & there,
            then gone, cut reckless

from their mooring.
When the men finally woke Him,
            he erased the names

of Heaven with his hand: Canaan,
Elysium, Kingdom of Incorruptible
                Crown.
He unfolded his palms
            into a compass of stars
as the pilgrims, lost,

marched into the sea.

When all he heard
        were the compressions

of waves against boat, He,
the pelican of piety, tore
                from His breast

enough flesh to feed the young.
His name was a stone
on their tongues, pulled
                        from a place
where light could never exist.

The Roman Room

The Roman Room

An image is, as it were, a figure, mark, or portrait of the object we wish to remember; for example, if we wish to remember a horse, a lion, or an eagle, we must place its image in a definite background.

—Cicero, Ad Herennium, III. XVI. 29-XVII.

We should therefore, if we desire to memorize a large number of items, equip ourselves with a large number of backgrounds, so that in these we may set a large number of images.

—Cicero, Ad Herennium, III. XVI. 29-XVII.

Begin with the intimate, what your hands have spent their lives
touching, naming: all those doors, windowpanes washed
      in stabs of black shadow.

Place your memories—one by one on each small surface,
each ledge & sill, until the room you've spent your whole life
      haunting
is filled with the simple architecture of images.

Let the destroyer be your backdrop, memory's palace,
where you first held the illusion of becoming a man,
      needing someone other than yourself.

You stood on the pier dressed in summer whites,
      the stranger
your wife had become holding the cuff of your sleeve, the sea
moving beneath your feet, her feet, the whole world
      empty and trembling.
Leave her here—motionless—against whitecaps,

47

        sea dust,
you in uniform, medals pinned to your chest, she with silk tied
in a knot to keep her hair from weaving a nest
        in your mouth.

Lay at her feet all the things that eventually leave:
        your father,
lost inside a deck of cards, hard galloping horses,
the score sheets of skinny dogs; your sister,
        lost
to the same inheritance: glass pipe pressed to her lips, yellow
flame set to city stones;
an uncle who wiped field dust from picture frames—
        bleached his sheets
& made his bed—before closing barn doors
& pushing
        a bullet through his head.

In the armory, among ammunition, stacks of black
        rifles, pistol clips,
place the image of your brother as you remember him: stoned,
asleep at the wheel, his rig drifting across the highway's
        dividing line,
Wyoming's sky green with hail. He told you once that the earth
        needs lightning

to nitrate fields, blacken soil, fertilize crops; everything
        you swallow, he said,
is made from explosions in the sky.
Set next to his image a human spine, the lightning that runs
        the length of our bodies;
remember him as reckless & necessary—a chewer of light.

Gather here, on the fantail, all the things you'll need
        for burials
at sea: casket, sailcloth, urn, podium & prayer book.
Remember the sucking sound the sea made
as Johnson's body was committed to the deep.

Remember, the sea shall give up her dead & the life
of the world to come.
        Place beside his sinking skin
offerings of flowers, ashes, small fires that float
on the surface, look like the sockets of a skull,
        whitening in the sun.

In the repair locker, place among the mauls, smoke curtains,
rip hammers, the image of your young wife
before she needed to feel
        the touch of other men.

Use the image of her before the war,
        you fingering
an engagement ring in your pocket on an unpeopled
beach off Lake Michigan. In the distance,
a dozen anchored boats —
        motionless
if not for the turning world — wind frozen in their sails.

Down to the ground on one knee — Yes.
Place here among the fire axes, cold chisels, all your great loves:
the blonde whose skin smelled of juniper, cigarette smoke,
        amphetamines —
ash from trailer park fires;
the medical student who diagnosed you with Soldier's Heart:
        a sickness of anger;

the cheap drunk with expensive dresses, perfumes,
        who swallowed jewels
of amber bourbon, rubies of wine.

In sick bay, where blades become bandages,
        where the knife heals,
place your pains, the hundred hurts a body sustains,
next to the stretchers and tourniquets, battle dressings,
        bone splints:

your mother, too poor to leave a country
you cannot pronounce, knee deep in the Black Sea,
        her blood
like watercolor in the quay, standing on the bayonets
of reefs, scrubbing piss from strangers' sheets.

On the shelf next to the burn kits, compression wraps,
place the things that have made you
        bleed:
the knife you paid a marine to sharpen, edge
with his leather belt, polish
        the blood groove
with spit and Skoal. When he's done, to show how sharp
he's honed the steel, he rests the blade
against his thumb, shaves off a flake of white nail so thin
        it carves the air like snow.

Place next to the fire rake & bolt cutters
the image of a harvest table—
your brother boring holes into a Red Delicious
        with a paring knife.

He loads the bowl with skunk weed, drops the turntable's
needle onto our father's warped copy
       of *Paint it Black.*
He opens the kitchen window, blows smoke
through the screen.
Outside, dusk unfolds,
& all you know is darkness: a black pond
swallowing its echo, —water entering water,
       rain erasing
topsoil, floating pea gravel to the surface: black pearls
of roe cut from the bellies of salmon.

Sober for years, your father keeps a knot
of stress in the crescent of his jaw,
               obvious as the throat of a king
snake swallowing. He clinches his teeth,
rocks bone against bone, massages the weight
with his fingers.
Picture a knot
anchored in the chambers of his heart.

& here, in your coffin rack,
where you keep your wife's perfumed letters, folded
uniforms, souvenirs of ruin,
place the image of a white hearse
careening down the Autobahn, Johnson's body in the back.
       You're his witness now; the ocean has survived
your swallowing.

Remember, you've written the equations by hand:
       Mass equals force over acceleration.
Calculate how fast the hearse must travel
          in order for Johnson's body to weigh nothing.

Throw into the ocean everything you wish to forget:
black rifles, your fingers turned to sand
        inside another's body;
the blood knot of your father's heart,
        finally untied. Throw into the sea
your broken tooth. Have faith that among the silt
& coral, it is the whitest stone.

Commit everything to memory: Here is your second wife,
standing ankle deep in a field
of trumpet flowers, tracing with her fingers
the shadow of a cross
        on the donkey's back.

Tell her this same beast stood at the foot of the crucifixion
cross until crows stole hair from the heads
of thieves.
Here is your father, casting an invisible line, a barbed hook
into the lake, shaped like a collapsed lung;
& here are your fingers in the ashes,
flames feeding your hands.

Retrace your steps. Everything is in its place:
Think of your father as the invisible
        line, all the unplowed acres of his pain.
Remember your wife as a thief, the heart
as nothing more than a blood noose that death unties.

Remember Johnson's body as cotton
inside the pillow of a body bag; remember the snow
that fell from your fingernails,
& the women you once loved: juniper and amphetemines,
sick heart, swallower of jewels.

Think of your first wife as a receding
          shoreline; think of your brother as a human
spine, chewer of light.

It's time to darken ship, to sleep. It's time to stand
behind the rifle, & guard the palace of your memory.

The Crying Room

Cayenne & Cinnamon

My grandmother remembers nothing
of her late husband but the gin-
blossom suspended above his coarse

white moustache, a map of broken
capillaries branching like tributaries
up & down the bridge of his nose.

Of her parents, even less:
the way her father's fingers smelled
of her mother's hair in the morning;

she combed rapeseed from the sleeves
of her father's work shirt with a comb.

In the kitchen, I mix cayenne, cinnamon
into a thick paste, rub the remedy
on both of her hands to deter her

from sucking her thumbs. An oral fixation,
the doctor assures us, is part of her
regression, one of many stages to come.

Last night she saw her brother—
dead twenty years from a lifetime
digging underground—entering her room

& stealing from the jewelry box
her alexandrite ring, silver brooch,
a shoebox full of costume jewelry
from the closet.

I want to believe her; then, no.
Here are her things as she left them:
cloudy jewels, rhinestones, polished glass,

all of them nesting in petite velvet
drawers: a boxful of chokers, bridals,
crystal pendants dumped on the floor.
She unbraids each shimmering strand,
searching for her rosary.

Field Nurse, 1862

If the ruts cut
by the weight of coffins

on the carriage
were to fill, let it be
          with water

clean enough to drink,
with light, or forgiveness.

If the men rolling
bread rations
      into rosary beads

were to pray, it would be
for birds, fifty-nine —

the number of feathers
in a wing, the number
      of bones in her hands.

She gathers their coats,
their blouses, the sleeves
& collars she holds

in her palms, feeling
        for a pulse.
The men, having never
    touched her,
but having turned the earth
    for graves, pour

something of themselves inside.
One soldier watches
    the field stitch together,

          hears angels sing
where cornstalks are cut,
piled, burned to black smoke.

Another cries out, & she cannot
feed him because the water
for washing is not for drinking.

Under threadbare canvas, over
porcelain bowls, she scrubs
    shit, blood from her dress,

strings the fabric between branches
to dry; a cloud of bees stings
the wind. Every night but tonight,

she squeezes her fingers into a fist,
touches the knot of her body:
the size of a heart, the shape
    of a horse's

hoof. She presses palm to palm,
prays: if this battlefield floods,
    let their rifles
be driftwood;

let the men believe all things
are boats, let them sign
their names
    in the spaces between stars.

Outside the walls of her tent,
she hears the echo of the cavalry,
steeds galloping off months of dust,
seeding the clouds with rain.

Waking

My grandmother collapses
her eyes in sleep,

dreams of the rusted
latticework of windmills,
their sails a monument

       to weather's ruin,
glare & fan of tin vanes
like a copper coin

dropped into the offering plate
of the pasture. Once, her land
      was all she knew:

the way tree limbs
shaped the wind's music,
      her husband's figure

crowning a slope of black
soil, swinging spark
      from his shaft lantern—

night entering the arrow
of the wick's flame, glint
      & swiveled

like a braid behind the glass
globe. Haunting,
      how even in sleep

she rows out to touch
the other side of light, *shadow*,
mouths the word for *home*.

So quiet, these nothing hours.
        A pool of summer
lifts from her hospice window,

the room dark enough to wake her,
the television's slight fire
        spilling into the hallway.

She sleeps to dream
        of her healthy body.
No longer do I imagine ascension

as a burning her body wakes to,
but the way a miner blindly walks
        the knots of rescue-rope.

Mawpin

My mother unfolds
his flannel
           in their room,

the cotton stinking
of potash
           & smoke,

to dress
the scarecrow
               convalesced

for months—mouth
unsewn, filled
           with stars—

in our field.
Mawpin. Bird-scarer,
           cruciform

at our barbwire fence.
His denim, too,
unwashed, untouched,

last year's soil
               lithographed
in both knees

from kneeling.
           They've returned,
the rooks & sparrows,

sensing absence,
the silence of his rifle.
          They've returned

to fat themselves
on his harvest.
          Outside, we knot

          the ankles,
tourniquet the sleeves,
stuff chaff & straw

into this father costume,
to guard against
a hunger he knew too well.

My Sister's Blindness

I have always known her eyes' desire to gather light. As a child, she lit a boxful of candles at the first sight of darkness, stood one in each window of the house, & blew out what was left of the flames in the morning. The night found its way to her room.

|

In 1572, the Treasury of Optics disproved the accepted belief that light pours from the eye, reaches outward to probe the world. The fact was recanted a year later, citing the use of cadaver eyes for dissection.

|

Diagnosed with childhood blindness, a permanent darkening of the world, she begged the devil to leave her body. The ophthalmologist told her that *Lucifer* translates to *light-bearer*. I prayed for her possession.

|

The Bible references the word eyes 502 times & the word *eyesight* once. Matthew 6:23: "But if your eyesight is bad, your whole body will be full of darkness. If then the light that is in you is darkness, how great is the darkness."

|

My mother ripped out every page of the bible that mentioned eyes or vision or sight. "We pray with our mouths, not our eyes," she said. The bible weighed the same, even with the pages missing.

|

Rene Descartes proved that the eye inverts the world—a camera obscura— by scraping away the back of an ox eye, placing it on the windowsill & watching the streets of Paris in the retina.

My sister has never been photographed with her eyes open; she says the sudden flash of light hurts.

|

In 1936, a prison warden in Omaha, Nebraska gave his death-row inmates the option of donating their eyes for transplant surgery after their execution, telling the World-Herald, "Where these men are going, they'll be grateful they can't see."

|

After a year in total darkness, she began pressing both thumbs into her eyes, saying she saw lakes of light. She pressed harder & saw shafts, splinters. Still harder, the light brightened enough to induce migraines. Her fingers left her eyelids a mess of yellow bruises. The optometrist split a ping-pong ball & taped halves over her eyes.

|

One day you'll be blind, like me. You'll be sitting there, a speck in the void, in the dark, forever, like me. —Samuel Beckett

|

My mother took my sister to the banks of the Mississippi River & told God to show himself. If He were real, He would bless the river & the water would wash away the darkness.

The Startle of the Sleeping World

The night not dark enough
to hide the blood dried
        black on the wings of geese,

my father, all day hunting,
gathers their broken necks,
                thick & awkward

as a bouquet of branches
in his fists. He bends
          at the hips, struggles

to drag their heavy bodies
into the light of the garage.
       He rummages his workbench

for a book of matches to light
the lantern, a whetstone to edge
        his boning knife.

Even now, my mind fills my eyes
with what the night hides:
           a sunburned body

wading knee-deep
          into every dark field,
windblown parchment

of the copperhead's molting,
the plow's rusted blade
         sparking float-stone.

Tonight, I'm awake to see
the world startle: birds littering
fencerows, scattering from the peal;

a collie trembling at the silver
buckle of a leather belt;
      a deer, wounded with arrows,

        bucking, then submitting
to the blade against its throat.
The garden too, set in motion:

camas bulbs turned by hand
in loose soil, water lily seeds
     from the pond, gray & round

as buckshot, heirloom tomatoes
split down the center, pregnant
    with pulp & spoil,

all paved over in spring with peat
stinking of sulfur & milkweed.
       Now, spider webs stretch

between the rake's tines, dust gathers
in the bowl of the shovel's blade,
work boots in the mudroom blacken
with soot from last year's fire

where we burned everything
we couldn't sell: mother's old bedsheets,
     dresses, patchwork quilts.

Acknowledgements

MEMORANDUM FOR THE RECORD: EVIDENCE/PROPERTY CUSTODY RECEIPT was first published in *Best New Poets: 50 Poems from Emerging Writers*

Shamal was first published in *elimae*

[Misreading] The Odyssey in Iraq was first published in *burntdistrict*

A Blind Date Asks About the War was first published in *Tupelo Quarterly*

Bow & Cello was first published in *Tahoma Literary Journal*

Jesus Dreamt Only Once was first published in *Ghost Ocean Magazine*

Cayenne & Cinnamon was first published in *Tar River Poetry Review*

Field Nurse, 1862 was chosen by Kelly Davio as a poetry winner of the Borges Prose and Poetry Prize and was first published in *Caper Literary Journal*

Mawpin was first published in *Gulf Stream Literary Magazine*

My Sister's Blindness was first published in *> kill author*

The Startle of the Sleeping World was first published in *Gargoyle*

Controlled Burn was first published, in a different form, in *Ghost Ocean Magazine*

Some poems in this book quote from, adapt, respond, or are otherwise indebted to B.H. Fairchild, Lt. Dave Bouve, Michael Loruss, Kerry James Evans, Hugh Martin, Larry Levis, Marvin Bell, Rebecca Hazelton, Jason Courtney, Neal Courtney, and everyone who labored to make these poems what they are. Thank you.

About the Author

Brandon Courtney was born and raised in Iowa, served four years (1999-2003) in the United States Navy (Operation Enduring Freedom), received his B.A. in English from Drake University in 2010, and his MFA from Hollins University in 2012. He is working towards an advanced degree at the University of Chicago.

www.ingramcontent.com/pod-product-compliance
Lightning Source LLC
Chambersburg PA
CBHW081539040426

42447CB00014B/3431